Udemy Marketing
A Step-By-Step Guide to Increasing Enrollment in Your Udemy Course

James Chen

Gamma Mouse

www.gammamouse.com

Introduction

When I published my first course on Udemy, I remember my excitement that people would now be able to enroll in my course, and hopefully gain something valuable from me. The thought of teaching my own course had always appealed to me, the idea of being able to share my knowledge with people around the world was incredibly exciting. Udemy allowed me to do this.

Once my course went live I figured students would soon start signing up. People would see the valued that my course offered, how what I was teaching could truly impact their lives. I waited patiently, refreshing my course statistics constantly, certain that my first student would register shortly. Days passed and I waited, my confidence started to fall. Soon after, weeks passed and it was clear that no one was interested in my course. It was frustrating. Despite all the hard work I invested in building my course, no one seemed interested. At first, I blamed my audience.

Don't they understand how valuable and amazing my course is? Slowly, I came to realize the truth: it was all my fault!

My first mistake was believing that just by publishing my course on Udemy students would be lining up to join. You need to give people a reason to spend their hard-earned money on your course, and I had not done that. I had a course—a great one, I thought—but there was no way for me to promote it. This shortcoming on my part taught me an incredibly valuable business lesson: behind every successful product is a successful promotion. If you want to sell anything, you need to have an audience to sell to. Many discover that getting an audience is the hardest part of any successful promotion. Either you need to tap into a new group of consumers or you have your own customer base to market your product to.

Marketing can be focused on gathering a new audience—or even better—maintaining and building your list of customers. Gathering a new audience is generally expensive as the cost per customer can be prohibitive. Many new businesses struggle with this because they don't have the funds available to acquire new customers. So retaining prior customers becomes extremely important. Starting out on Udemy, you will need to find an audience of prospective students, unless you have prior leads, and you will want student acquisition to be cost-effective. This guide will outline an inexpensive method for attracting students to your courses. I will show you how to tap into a huge audience that is eager to sample your product no matter the subject matter.

But before we begin, let me tell you what this guide will not cover. Time will not be spent on the details of designing and publishing your course on Udemy. This is not an step-by-step guide to getting started on Udemy; there are other books better suited to this task. This guide will assume that you already have a course available—or soon to be available—on Udemy, and you are searching for a promotional strategy that is effective and can be implemented quickly. With this in mind, my goal is to keep the explanation of this method short, giving you the immediate knowledge you need in order to implement it as soon as possible. I have always hated searching through pages of text in order to find the actionable items that I needed. Sometimes brevity is necessary, and I believe this is one of those times. The time saved here will be better used to promote your Udemy course.

One final thing to mention before we get started. Years ago, a friend of mine—who was an incredibly successful internet marketing guru—gave me a copy of his notes that outlined his best strategies for making money online. This guide had been an invaluable marketing resource for me over the years, and I would like to offer it to you for free as a way to pay it forward. Before you start reading, I invite you to download your free copy at http://gammamouse.com/quit_your_job.

Overview of the Process

To start, I want to present an overview of the entire Udemy marketing strategy that I will cover in this guide. Some readers—who may be experienced in internet marketing—may only need to read this chapter to understand the general strategy, and can begin implementing these ideas immediately. For everyone else, be advised that I will explain each step of the process in more detail in subsequent chapters. So don't worry if this overview doesn't make sense now, I promise it will by the end of this book.

Step One - Develop an e-book by either re-purposing existing course material, writing new material, or outsourcing to a freelancer. The text should be between 3000 and 5000 words, and the subject matter should be the same as your course. Additionally, design a cover yourself or outsource it to a designer.

Step Two - Create a coupon code on Udemy that will give users access to your course for free.

Step Three - Generate the coupon link and place it in your book's introduction. Inform your readers that the code offers them free access to your course which will provide them with much more information.

Step Four - Publish your book to Amazon, Google Play, Apple Store, Barnes & Noble, Kobo, and others. (Apple Store, Barnes & Noble, Kobo and other retailers are accessed by publishing through either Smashwords or Draft2Digital.) Set the price of your book to free at every retailer except Amazon. (We need the book to be free in these sales channels first before Amazon will price match.) Email Amazon Kindle Direct Publishing support asking them to price match once your book has been priced for free at other outlets.

Step Five (optional) - Repeat steps one through four as desired. Publishing additional books will reach even more buyers, many of which will use the coupon code to enroll in your course.

Step Six - When you are satisfied with your course enrollment, replace the coupon link in your book—or books. Continue to link to your course, though. You can still offer a discount code if you wish, or you can ask for the full price. I've found offering a 50% off coupon to be the most effective. I price my Udemy course with this in mind.

Once again, don't worry if these steps aren't clear to you right now. I will examine each of these steps in more detailed in the coming chapters. Once you are finished with this book, you may find it useful to refer back to this overview to help you through the process. Now that we have a roadmap, let's examine each of these steps more thoroughly.

Step By Step Explanation of the Process

Step One

Our first step is to produce an e-book that is related to our Udemy course. Don't worry; this is actually simpler than it sounds. We need a topic to start, and it needs to be highly relevant to your course. For example, if you are offering a Udemy course about managing your money, you will want your book to be about managing your money. Simple, right? This is a great way of drawing the audience that you are looking for to your course. If you produce a book whose subject matter is unrelated to your course, you are less likely to interest people in signing up for your course. Got it? Let's move on!

There are a few ways that you can produce your e-book: write 3000-5000 words yourself on the topic, use already developed course materials and re-package them as an e-book, or outsource the book to a freelance writer. Obviously, writing the book yourself will be the most time-consuming, while outsourcing it will be the most expensive. You will have to make the decision what you value more—your time or your money. If you decide to write an original book, all you will need to do is produce a document in your favorite word processing program of at least 3000 words.

If you already have course material that would work, then re-packaging it into a 3000 word book is the easiest solution. The downside is that those that have read the book will already have a small portion of your course. This isn't too much of a problem, because the video lessons are the real big selling point in any Udemy course.

Outsourcing is the tactic I use most often since I value my time. I would rather spend that time making a new Udemy course rather than writing an e-book. My favorite sites for outsourcing material are elance.com, upwork.com, and iWriter.com, all of which are fantastic for getting assignments written quickly. You can usually get a small book written in a week, and many times even faster than that. Generally, I don't spend more than $30 on a writing project as it tends to offer the best return. Spending more means it might take longer to break even on your marketing, particularly if you produce multiple e-books in order to promote your Udemy course.

A word of caution if you decide to outsource your e-book: always check for plagiarism using an online tool like copyscape.com. Though most of the freelancers you will deal with are honest and hard-working, there are the occasional bad apples that will try to pass off an article they found on the Internet as their original work. Amazon checks any book submitted for content that is freely available online, and will not publish it unless you are also the author of the online content. Now that you know, there shouldn't be any surprises if this comes up in the publishing process. Still, the best way to avoid this is to check anything written for you with an online plagiarism detector.

We still need a cover for our e-book before we can move on to the next step. I usually outsource this, too, since I'm not a designer. If you have the skills to design a cover, feel free to tackle it yourself. If you want someone else to do it, I highly recommend going to fiverr.com, and using one of the top-rated book cover designers. Most of them do outstanding work, and will produce a professional-looking cover in only a couple of days. Look around and I certain you will find a designer who appeals to your aesthetic. Before you order have the following information about your book close at hand: the title, the subtitle (if you have one, but I recommend it), and the author's name. You don't have to use your name if you don't want to; a pen name is completely fine. Some designers will ask you for links to book covers that you like. This can be accomplished with a quick Amazon search, and copying the links of books with covers you really like.

Now that we know the avenues available to us for producing an e-book, it is time to take action and do it. Once you have your e-book written, you can move on to Step Two.

Step Two

Now that the hard part is behind us, we can concentrate on putting a few finishing touches on our book before we publish it. With that in mind, step two is the easiest step in the process. All you need to do is go onto Udemy and create a coupon code and link for your course. The coupon should offer the course at a 100% discount, so your readers will be able to enroll for free.

Some of you might be complaining: why should I allow them free access to the course I worked so hard on. The simple answer: we want to increase the number of students enrolled so we can appear to other Udemy shoppers to be an extremely popular course. Think of it as building up your social proof. If an individual searching Udemy sees two similar courses, one with an enrollment of 2 students versus another which has 2000 students, which one do you think they are more likely to sign up for. Social proof—it is what separates the money-making Udemy classes from the rest. Don't worry, though. Once we have achieved our enrollment goal, we are going to discontinue the coupon code. Usually when I hit the student enrollment I want, I will change my codes to offer a much smaller discount— usually no less than 50% off.

I know giving away your work for free can feel counter-intuitive, but it is amazing how much money you can earn by giving information away for free. I have offered free products in a variety of online situations, and they have all produce positive cash flow, many times beyond what I could have envisioned. I hope I have convinced you enough to give it a try; you will be happily surprised with the results.

Now that we have our coupon link, we are going to place it in our newly created e-book for Step Three.

Step Three

Ready to finally finish setting up your e-book? The finish line is definitely in sight. Our last item to do is to write an introduction to our e-book. We want to keep this super simple. In my introductions, I thank the reader for downloading my book, and then give a brief overview of what the book will cover. From there, I transition into promoting my Udemy course.

Usually, I inform my reader that I have developed a Udemy course that is a companion to the guide, which offers even more information than they will find in my book. I will highlight how I go much more in-depth in the videos for my course. And then I hit them with the best part. Because I want my readers to succeed, I am offer free access to my course for a limited time only. I inform them that they can take advantage of this special opportunity by using the following coupon link, before finishing with the link. It's really that simple, yet incredibly effective.

Once you have finished up the introduction, it is time to get your e-book formatted properly. Again I use fiverr.com and pay someone to format my book for me. I suggest you look for a formatter who will take your document, format it, and return it to you as an .epub. Because we are going to be submitting our book to multiple sources, the .epub format will make our lives much easier since all the sources I suggest to you will accept that format.

Once your book has been returned to you in the .epub format, we are now ready for Step Four—publishing our book!

Step Four

Publishing our book is actually quite simple. You already should have the .epub format, the cover, the title, subtitle, and author's name. You are also going to want to write a description for you book. I suggest at least 100 words for your description, though it isn't terribly important since we are going to be offering our e-book for free. Once you have everything together, it is time to publish.

Amazon should be your first stop, since it is the largest e-book retailer. You will need a Kindle Direct Publishing account which you can sign up for at https://kdp.amazon.com/. It is completely free to publish your book. Retailers take a percentage only when you sell a book. Once you have logged in, you will click on the "Create new title". You will then fill in all the title, subtitle, description, and author information as well as upload your epub and cover. There is a box at the top of the first page which asks if you want to enroll in KDP Select. Do not select this, as we don't want to be exclusively limited to selling on Amazon. If you accidentally enroll in KDP Select, don't worry you can cancel your enrollment within three days. Just make sure you aren't enrolled.

Once you have entered all of the pertinent information and submitted the first page, you will be taken to the pricing page. There is a lot less information that needs to be filled out here. Amazon won't let you offer your book for free; it needs to have a price. We will eventually get our book priced free at Amazon by asking for a price match. My personal preference is to select the 70% commission button and enter $4.99 as the price for my book. The reason for this is that when Amazon does price match your book when it goes free, it will cross out the $4.99 price. Having a higher price point supposedly encourages more downloads since readers will perceive that they are getting a more valuable book for free. I'm not convinced this is true, but it is something to consider when pricing your book. Just don't price it higher than $9.99.

Once you have set your price, you are all done—it is time to publish your book. Hit the publish button, and within 24 hours your book should be available on Amazon. Pretty simple, right?

Even though Amazon has a huge slice of the e-book market, we want to upload our book now to the other big e-book retailers like Apple, Barnes & Noble, Kobo, and Google Play since these retailers allow us to price our book for free. Don't worry, though, we are going to use Draft2Digital.com to simplify the process. When you upload your book on Draft2Digital, you are able to simultaneously publish your book to Apple, Barnes & Noble, and Kobo as well as other smaller sites which we are going to skip. Sign up for an account at Draft2Digital.com, and click on the "Add New Book" button. The publishing process is similar to Amazon; you will fill out the title, author, and description as well as upload your epub and cover. The final step will be the pricing page. You want to enter $0.00 in the pricing field and check the boxes next to the following retailers: Apple, Barnes & Noble, and Kobo. Leave the others blank since not all of the sites allow you to sell your book for free.

Finally, you want to publish your book on Google Play. You can sign up for an account at https://play.google.com/books/publish/. You should have no problem with the publishing process now that you have used both Amazon and Draft2Digital.

You will likely have to wait a few days for each of the retailers to make your book available. Draft2Digital will email you when you book is published to each platform. There will be a link in these emails that you will want to copy and save, since you will need them when you ask Amazon for a price match. As for Google Play, you will want to go to your account, click on "Book Catalog", and then click on the title of your book. Then click on the "Content" tab on the menu bar. You will notice a link that says "Google Play". If you click on this it will take you to your book. Copy the link and save it with the ones you have for Apple, Kobo, and Barnes & Noble.

Once you have the links to your book on Google Play, Apple, Kobo, and Barnes & Noble, you are ready to email Amazon support and ask for a price match. Before you do, check that your book is free on each of these other sites; you don't want to email Amazon and give them a link to your book on another site where it isn't free. Now that you are ready, go to your Kindle Direct Publishing account, and click on "Help" at the top. Now scroll down the help page until you see the "Contact Us" button at the bottom. Press it. Now select "Pricing & Royalties", and then "Price Matching".

In your message, you want to tell Kindle support that your book is free at competing retailers, and that you would like Amazon to match it. Paste the links to your books on Google Play, Apple, Kobo, and Barnes & Noble into the message. Within 24 hours, Amazon support should respond. There are a few ways they can respond. One of the responses may ask for more time to check out the information you sent them. Other responses may state that they have price matched your book and it will show up in their system within a few days. While it has never happened to me, I have heard of others who were refused the price match. If this happens, check that your book is free on Google Play, Apple, Barnes & Noble, and Kobo. If it isn't free, make the change through either Draft2Digital or Google Play.

If you don't see a problem, email Amazon support again as I outlined above. It is important you include the links to your book on the other sites. Eventually, if you email support asking for a price match, you will find a support person who will match it. So don't give up!

Once Amazon has price matched your book, it is considered perma-free. In other words, as long as it remains free at other outlets, it will remain free on Amazon. You did it, give yourself a pat on the back. From that point forward, customers will be able to download your book for free.

Steps Five and Six

Now that our book is free across multiple retailers, how many students should we expect to enroll in our Udemy course? This is hard to predict. It will be dependent on the topic of your book and course, how many people download it for free, and the quality of your offer. At worse, you should expect somewhere between 1 to 5 percent of people who downloaded your book to sign up for your course. So the key is to get as many people to download your book as possible. Here is how I tackle this problem—publish more books using the exact process we went through above. More books mean more downloads, which mean more opportunities, and more students. The more books you publish, the faster you will hit your enrollment goals, and start to make serious money. And when you no longer wish to give away free access to your course, you can replace the coupon link in your book with one that either offers no discount or a minor one. These books will be your best marketing tool, whether they are used to build up your initial enrollment, or whether they are used to bring in potentially paying customers. The bottom line is that they bring traffic to your Udemy course; it is up to you to figure out the best way to maximize that traffic.

I hope you've found this guide helpful. This process has worked well for me, and has served as a big portion of my marketing efforts. I hope it benefits you, too!

WAIT! Before You Leave…

Download the #1 Bestseller from Gamma Mouse Media for FREE! Hurry this offer won't last as it is for a limited time only. Reserve your free copy today at http://gammamouse.com.

A Special Gift for Our Readers!

Thank you so much for your purchase of this book. As a special gift for you we have included one of our bestselling Self-Improvement books: Procrastination: Triple Your Productivity and Accomplish Your Goals written by one of the most well-respected and influential experts on time management, Warren R. Sullivan.

I hope you enjoy!

Procrastination

Triple Your Productivity and Accomplish Your Goals

Warren R. Sullivan

Gamma Mouse

www.gammamouse.com

PROCRASTINATION
Copyright © 2014 by Warren R. Sullivan.
All rights reserved.

First Edition: April 2014
1234567890
A Gamma Mouse eBook
Published by Gamma Mouse, a dba of Xilytics, LLC.
www.gammamouse.com

Introduction

Procrastination. It has a drastic effect on productivity, on our ability to accomplish our goals in life. It can greatly impact our happiness, as we avoid doing something that we are dreading. Yet having to do it still hangs over our head.

Delaying something in order to often do something easier is an easy trap to fall into. Do it enough, and it suddenly becomes a habit. The problem with procrastination is we usually put off more important—but also more difficult—objectives for doing actions that are more trivial. For example, a college student might watch television rather than write a report.

Our time is valuable. It is the one thing that cannot be replaced, unlike money or objects. Yet it is wasted when we procrastinate. Saving this time should be our goal. We need to realize that our time would be better spend on accomplishing our most important objectives. When you have finished those, then reward yourself.

Stopping our procrastination is as easy as changing our attitude and stopping the habit that we have fallen into. In reading this guide, you will learn the tips and tricks necessary to stop procrastinating and start living. You don't have to suffer any longer, you can be happy and more productive, accomplishing all the important goals in your life quickly and easily. But you must take the first step and make a commitment to change yourself. Reading this book is a start, but if you don't act on what you learn change will not come. So consider this a call to action, a chance to truly change your life.

Getting to the root of the problem

Everyone procrastinates. It is part of being human. Whether because of laziness or not having the energy to tackle a difficult task, we choose to relax, to take the easy way out. Understand that not all procrastination should be viewed as bad. Often we need a break from the rigors of our day, a chance to get away from the stress of life. Some goals require great effort and energy to complete, so tackling them when you don't have much energy is realistic.

The line we don't want to cross is when we fool ourselves into believing that laziness is not having the energy to complete our task. Our first step is to recognize when we are being lazy. Clearly, we need to be honest with ourselves, we need to hold ourselves accountable. Secondly, we need to realize that time is our most valuable resource, and that it is finite. No one knows how much time they have, so it is essential to understand how important time is. When you sit down to watch television, recognize that this is time you will never get back.

To borrow a phrase from economics, understand that there is an opportunity cost to ever action you take. When you choose to do something, you lose the opportunity to use that time differently. When you make a choice, there is always a cost, remind yourself of this when you find yourself procrastinating. One of my methods for reminding myself to utilize every minute of my time as effectively as I can is to write the number 1440 on the white board in my office. This is the number of minutes in one day. Whenever I find myself procrastinating, I look at my board, and it helps me refocus on my task at hand.

People procrastinate for different reasons. The first step is to understand the reasoning behind our procrastinating. There may be more than one, but understanding the psychology behind our choices will help us effectively combat them, allowing us to change our faulty reasoning when it arises.

Cognitive distortions are a form of irrational thinking that often lead to procrastination. It is a magically type of thinking. Often we believe that we will be better equipped at some point in the future to handle our task, rather than completely the task at that time.

An example is a person who believes that they need to be in a certain mood in order to complete a task successfully. Or a person may believe that their motivation will increase in the future, and thus will be in a better position to accomplish their goals. Another one that happens in business quite frequently is an employee overestimating the time they have left to complete a task while also underestimating how long it will take them to do it.

If you are putting off a task, because you believe that you will be better suited in the future, realize that you are committing a fallacy. There is no evidence suggesting that your belief is true.

When we are confused about how to complete a task, and the details involved, we may procrastinate giving the reason that we need further instructions before we can continue. This allows us to set the project aside, until we find that we are butting up against a deadline. This reasoning often comes up with perfectionists who do not want to start a task until they are confident in their ability to complete it perfectly. To combat this reasoning, understand that completely the task initially to the best of your abilities and understanding, and then waiting for feedback is much more productive. It is easy to make corrections to your mistakes once the task is completed, as opposed to trying to do the task perfectly the first time. And there is always the possibility that the goal will be accomplished on your first attempt, without the need for further clarification. Don't fool yourself into thinking that if you have additional information, you will be better suited to complete the task. This is a cognitive distortion.

An offshoot of this is avoiding a task because you don't know how it should be done, that you require procedural information. Once again, this reasoning arises most often in the perfectionist, who believes they need to wait for the perfect situation in order to be successful. But look at the great inventors throughout history, who only through trial and error found out how to accomplish something amazing. Imagine if they had waited for the perfect moment, these inventions may never have come into existence. Remember that your goal is to accomplish your task, mistakes that you make can always be corrected. Don't fear failure. Instead, recognize it as an opportunity to learn.

I used to suffer from thinking I needed to take the time, to contemplate and reflect, before beginning a job. What I was doing was procrastinating, convincing myself I needed more information. This was clearly a logical fallacy. Thinking about the job was not going to make me more productive. What was going to make me more productive was doing it. If you believe you need more time to accomplish something, stop and examine whether that is true. Even if it is true, you can start the task now and revise it later as your thoughts begin to coalesce.

We have all had tasks that we had to do that we really didn't want to do. Income taxes come to mind. It is a responsibility, and sometimes that additional pressure makes a task unpleasant. And we are human, we do not want to do things we find unpleasant. We may even fool ourselves into thinking that there will be a point in the future when it will be easier to deal with an unpleasant task. Never make the mistake to think that a task that is unpleasant today will somehow miraculously improve in the future. It is always better to get the unpleasantness over immediately, rather than wait. I am reminded of my public speaking class in college. I always wanted to go first, and I could never understand why people wouldn't want to be first. Most found public speaking uncomfortable and unpleasant, but instead of immediately getting it out of the way and then relaxing, they chose to prolong how long the task would take them. Don't fall victim to this. If you find a task unpleasant, do it immediately; procrastination only makes it worse, and in the process makes you unhappy.

Now the opposite of procrastinating over tasks that we find unpleasant is to procrastinate over accomplishing goals that we don't care about. Finding the effort to complete a task when you are indifferent to the outcome is difficult. Often we may believe that we will feel more inclined to complete a task in the future when we feel more connected with the outcome. Usually indifference does not change, people don't suddenly start to care. These types of tasks often don't get tackled until we run up against a deadline. This can cause us additional stress as we must now take time to complete a task we don't care about instead of tasks that are much more important to us. Understand the cost of procrastinating may not be felt until the future when the task must be completed. Completing the task immediately saves you from future repercussions that you cannot anticipate.

I previously relayed the example of people believing that at some point in the future they will be in a better mood to accomplish a task. They may believe that certain moods make them more productive and believe that they need to wait for when they are in that mood. Recognize that this is an irrational reason you are giving yourself in order to procrastinate. While your emotions can affect your work, this is only generally in the case of extremes. Slight fluctuations in mood will have no effect, so don't convince yourself that you will be in a better mood to complete the task in the future. There is no truth to this.

A more specific example of this idea that a certain mood is essential for higher productivity is the case of individuals who wait until the last moment to start a task. The student who begins to study for mid-terms the night before the text, or the employee who starts an project the day before it is due are two examples of this. Waiting until the last minute to start because you think you are more productive up against a deadline is nothing more than believing that your mood makes you more productive at a point in the future. Don't fall for this procrastination excuse.

An additional reason you don't want to wait until you are up against a deadline is the cognitive distortion in which you overestimate the time you have while underestimating how long it will take you to accomplish a task. If you wait, believing you work better under pressure, you may place yourself in a situation in which you have significantly underestimated the time you will need. This may cause you to rush, resulting in sub-standard work. Or, even worse, you may miss your deadline completely. Avoid backing yourself into this corner where time works against you. Remember that we often believe that we have more time than we actually do.

Another reason people often give for procrastinating is that they had forgotten about a job. Often the reason that it was forgotten is intentional, the task may be unpleasant or one that we are indifferent about. If a deadline is far into the future, it can be easy to forget about our upcoming responsibilities. Or we may believe that we will get to it closer to the deadline. Understand that this is procrastination, and that there is nothing keeping you from completing the job now.

The final cognition distortion I will address is the belief that you don't want to currently complete a job because you are not feeling well, and that you will wait until you feel better. It should be evident how this is very similar to waiting for a specific mood in order to complete a task. Understand that there is no guarantee that you will feel better, in fact, you may end up feeling worse. Granted that people suffer from real health problems that greatly impact their ability to be productive. This is not what I am referring to. Instead, I refer to procrastinators who exaggerate how they feel to shirk their responsibilities. Don't be disingenuous with yourself about how you feel in order to avoid doing something.

Many of these cognition distortions are rooted in perfectionism or in our fear. We are either waiting for the moment to be right, or we are waiting to overcome our fear to do a task we may find unpleasant. Tell yourself that the moment will never be perfect, but it will be good enough to get the job done. Or if you are dealing with fear, realize that confronting your fear and doing the job now, will mean that once you have finished you will no longer have anything to fear. In fact, you will likely feel elated. This is a much better situation to be in than living under a cloud of dread.

Now that we have explored the underlying psychological reasons behind procrastination, our attention will turn to effective methods for dealing with procrastination. By employing the appropriate methods to our life, we will be able to become happier and more productive people.

Recognize the problem

Like with any addiction or problem, the first step is always to recognize and accept that you have a problem. Since you have purchased this book, I will assume that you have identified yourself as a procrastinator, and are now taking the proper steps to remedy this.

Do not feel shamed or embarrassed, identifying and attacking your problems is a noble and brave action. Focus on your self-awareness; stopping procrastination means keeping a keen eye on your behaviors. And making the necessary corrections.

Exercise

I want you to exam your behavior and thought processes. Write down three incidents in which you procrastinated.

Refer to the previous chapter if you want to show why your reasoning was faulty.

Find the root of the problem

Why are you procrastinating? Are you a perfectionist? Is fear keeping you from accomplishing certain tasks? Be honest with yourself. Discovering the root of your procrastination is important. If you recognize the cognition distortions that you are employing, this will give you a hint at the root of your procrastination. While knowing the underlying cause is helpful, identifying your faulty reasoning so you can correct it will have greater long-term gains.

If you are a perfectionist or if fear is holding you back, I want you to take a moment and examine your thinking. Why do you have to be perfect? Does it make you more productive? Does it make you happier? My guess is the answer will be "no". Tell yourself that accomplishing something perfectly is not the goal, the goal is only accomplishing your task. Withhold judgment, jobs are either done or not done. Also, ask yourself is it true that the longer you wait, the closer you will be to perfect? Or would you have done the same job either way? Does the evidence actually support your way of thinking?

The same approach can be taken if you suffer from fear. Ask yourself what you are afraid of? Most people fear a specific outcome. Is it rational to believe that outcome is guaranteed? I may fear dying in a plane crash, so I dread getting on a plane. But what are the chances that this event actually occurs. My chances are much greater of dying in a car accident on the way to the airport, but I don't have the same dread getting into a car. By nature, fear is not rational; it often arises from the fact that we have convinced ourselves of a terrible outcome, even though that outcome may be incredibly remote. Try to look at your fear rationally; assess the likelihood of the outcomes you fear. Then ask yourself: is it really that bad? Surprisingly, our fears are often overstated; they have a tendency to shrink when we look at them rationally.

Exercise

Using the previous chapter, identify any cognitive distortions you have fallen victim to. Can you discern what is behind this? If it is fear or the desire to be perfect, look at potential outcomes. Does it really need to be perfect? Is it a situation that you should be fearful of? Write down the reasons why you believe you need to be perfect, or write down why you should be afraid. Put it away for a day, and then read it again. Do your thoughts appear logical?

Prioritize with lists

Writing down a list is very effective in helping you achieve your goals. But you need to stick with it. Many people write lists, and then don't follow them. Remember the list is to help you stop procrastinating. Once you write the list, don't convince yourself out of following the order you set.

Put the jobs in order of priority, the most important being first and the least important being last. Estimate how long you believe each task will take you. Then multiply that time by a factor of three. Set this revised time as your deadline. The extra time will take into account the possibility that you are underestimating how long each task will take you; it serves as a buffer. The benefit is that if you complete your tasks early, you now have that extra time to do things you want to.

Keep your list close at hand. You can either write it down, or like I do, keep it on a mobile device.

There are numerous to-do list apps that will simplify the process.

Exercise

Write a list in which you prioritize your tasks by level of importance. Decide how long it will take you to do each task, then multiply that number by three. Write down the time needed next to each task on your list.

Divide and conquer

There are some tasks that are so large and unwieldy that estimating how long they will take is an incredibly difficult job. To help facilitate the process, break the large job into smaller segments. These segments should be small enough that you can estimate the time each one of them will take. Make certain you add in a buffer by multiplying each estimated time by three.

If you have a specific deadline, you can now add the time estimations for each of the smaller tasks to arrive at a figure for the entire project. This is a fantastic way to estimate large projects without placing yourself in a stressful situation as the deadline approaches. In fact, this approach is used quite frequently in the software industry for large multi-team projects.

Exercise

If you have a large project on your list, particularly if you are having difficulty estimating how long it will take, break it down into smaller segments. Now evaluate how much time each task will take, keeping the added buffer in mind.

Keep distractions to a minimum

One of the biggest productivity killers in recent years for businesses has been the Internet. It becomes easier for employees to procrastinate when they have other options that are more appealing only a mouse click away. With social media and email, there is always something new happening, and it can be quite difficult not to get immersed in this flow of constant information.

There are productivity plugins that will limit your access to the Internet by allowing you to stay online for short periods of time. If possible, I also recommend shutting down your email program, and only checking it at designated times. One method that is effective is to focus on your task for the first 50 minutes in the hour. In the remaining ten minutes, you can then check your email or Facebook status.

Additionally, a work or home environment can be distracting. People talking, a television playing, and other background noise can make you lose your focus. Listening to music through headphones or using earplugs is effective in blocking out distracting noise.

Exercise

Are you being distracted? Analyze your environment and decide whether you are being distracted. If you find yourself going online to check email or surf the Internet, try to use the 50 minute rule. Browser plugins will also limit your access to the Internet. Research, install, and configure them if you need this level of restriction.

If noise is a problem, buy earplugs or bring your headphones and MP3 player in order to listen to music.

Celebrate your accomplishments

You have completed your task list; time to celebrate. Giving yourself a reward after accomplishing your goals is wonderful way to encourage yourself to leave procrastination behind. The reward can be anything, an hour of television, a movie and dinner out, or an item you want. The point is to make it something you really desire, to properly give you a sense of accomplishment.

Exercise

Schedule a reward for yourself for completing your task list. Make it good. You deserve it.

Take care of yourself

Eating right and sleeping the recommended amount by your physician is essential in helping to reduce stress and anxiety. It is much easier to tackle your task list if you are feeling energized after a good night's sleep followed by a substantial breakfast. Often poor eating habits during the day lead to your blood sugar crashing in the afternoon, leaving you feeling sluggish and tired.

Make a point of eating a balanced diet spread over at least three meals over the course of the day. Maintain a regimented sleeping schedule. Try to go to bed and wake up at approximately the same time every day. Maintaining our sleep rhythms is very important.

Exercise, put it as a high priority on your task list if you have to. This can be as simple as taking a short walk. Exercising has the wonderful effect of increasing your energy, so take advantage.

Exercise

Evaluate your eating and sleeping habits, making the necessary changes. If you are not exercising, start. It can be as simple as a thirty minute walk per day.

Learn to say no

Many of us have the tendency to want to please other people. We take on more tasks and responsibilities than we have time for, causing us to have too many things to accomplish and not enough time to do them in. If you become too overwhelmed, there is a very good chance you will procrastinate rather than tackle your enormous list.

Learning to say no to task of low importance is key. When someone asks you to do something, look at what they are asking objectively. Is this task a high priority to you? What is the opportunity cost to you? Remember that your time is extremely valuable, it cannot be replaced. Time you spend on this task could be spent elsewhere. Unless it is a close family member, the most time I'm willing to spend on a task for someone is ten minutes. If I don't think I can accomplish it in ten minutes (after adding in my buffer), I will apologize and tell the person that I can't do it. Most people understand, they realize that we all lead busy lives. And if they don't, it is only further justification that I made the right decision.

Exercise

Look at your task list. Are there low priority jobs on it that you agreed to do for other people? If so, remove them from your list and let the person know, unless you believe you can accomplish it in a very short timeframe.

Be proactive in obtaining the information you need

During our examination of cognition distortions, we talked about procrastinating because we lack specific information about how to proceed or what our ultimate goal was. The way to avoid this problem is to always ask questions immediately on being given the task. Make certain you understand what your deliverables will be as well as the best way to proceed. There is no harm in asking and getting the answer. It will save you both time and aggravation.

With the advent of cellphones and email, people are generally accessible within a few hours. If the person you need to ask is not available, try to ask someone who has completed a similar task. Asking questions is not only an effective method for curtailing procrastination, it also has a generally positive affect on your life. We live in a society where the majority of people ask too few questions.

Exercise

Examine your task list. Is there a task that you have questions about? If so, contact the person who can answer your questions immediately. Even if it is late, send them an email. Don't wait, act on your questions right now.

Get into the habit

Procrastination is a bad habit, emphasis on habit. Habits need to be broken, and the best way to accomplish this is by replacing them with a new habit. If you have taken the suggested action to this point, you have already started on your way to replacing your habit to procrastinate. But it is only the start. Generally, it is believed that if a person can change their behavior for twenty-one days that change will become permanent.

Exercise

Find a calendar and mark off twenty-one days from today. Your goal is to keep up on doing your task list daily for the twenty-one days. Be aware that you will have to fight to keep procrastination from coming back in. Replacing old habits can be difficult, which means you need to remain vigilant of any back-sliding.

Make tasks relevant to you

Many of the jobs we do are done despite us being indifferent to the task or not enjoying it. The easiest way to combat this is to look at the task and accentuate a positive aspect of it. If you can find a good reason for doing something, it will make accomplishing it much more attractive to you. Think outside the box for reasons if you have to. Maybe completing a task will open up a new opportunity in your life, or allow you to connect with different people. Accomplishing it may give you the opportunity to make new friends.

There are a variety of reasons why a task should be completed. You need to find the one that holds the most appeal to you.

Exercise

Take a moment to examine your list. Are there any jobs you do not enjoy to do? Are there any tasks you feel indifferent about? If so, think of a good reason, one that appeals to you, of what completing the task could mean for you. Try to find a reason that makes you want to tackle the job.

Conclusion

I hope that you have found this journey helpful. If you have participated in the recommended exercises along the way, you should be commended. You have clearly decided you want to change, and that is a huge first step to becoming a more productive person.

Procrastination is not something you need to suffer with, the answers are all right here in this guide. Understand that procrastination can have deep psychological roots, causes that take time and effort to overcome. The best way to accomplish this is to face it head on. If you are a perfectionist, try completing a task even though you may not feel it is perfect, or up to your usual standards. If fear is holding you back, stand up to it by imagining the worst outcome, and then honestly evaluating how likely that outcome will come to be.

Humans suffer from many irrational thoughts, convinced of the truth of an idea even though the evidence suggests the opposite. Recognizing these irrational thoughts is the first step in dispelling them. Once you realize you are being illogical, the thought fails to hold any power over you anymore. Never take anything for granted, continuously question your thoughts, assessing them for validity. This isn't only the key to stopping procrastination, it also leads to a life that is happier and more productive.

I wish you all the success in your journey.

WAIT! Before You Leave…

www.ingramcontent.com/pod-product-compliance
Lightning Source LLC
Chambersburg PA
CBHW070942180526
45168CB00003B/1150